How to Build
the Ghost in Your Attic

Also by Peter Jay Shippy:

Alphaville
(BlazeVOX Books, 2006)

Thieves' Latin
(Iowa Poetry Prize Winner, University of Iowa Press, 2003)

How to Build
the Ghost in Your Attic

a book-length poem by
Peter Jay Shippy

Rose Metal Press

2007

Rose Metal Press
P.O. Box 1956
Brookline, MA 02446
rosemetalpress@gmail.com
www.rosemetalpress.com

Library of Congress Control Number: 2007936239

ISBN: 978-0-9789848-2-3

Book design by Rebecca Krzyzaniak.
See "A Note About the Type" for typeface information.

This book is manufactured in the United States of America and printed on acid-free paper.

Credit: The epigraph is from *Ghost Trio* by Samuel Beckett. Copyright © 1975 by the Estate of Samuel Beckett. Originally appeared in *Ends and Odds* (Grove Press, 1975). Reprinted by permission of Georges Borchardt, Inc. on behalf of the Estate of Samuel Beckett.

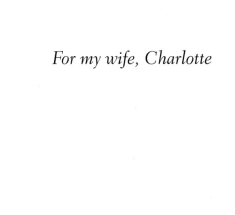

For my wife, Charlotte

32. *Cut to near shot of small boy full length in corridor before open door. Dressed in black oilskin with hood glistening with rain. White face raised to invisible F. 5 seconds. Boy shakes head faintly. Face still, raised. 5 seconds. Boy shakes head again. Face still, raised. 5 seconds. Boy turns and goes. Sound of receding steps. Register from same position his slow recession till he vanishes in dark at end of corridor. 5 seconds on empty corridor.*

—Samuel Beckett, *Ghost Trio*

1

I am Isaac Makepeace Watt—
    the lamb
      of light.

Believe you me.
    In the lees
      of October I'm sinking like Venice, like a lob, lolling
a beanbag odalisque
      in my attic rental, masturbating
         to my favorite comic book—

         $@#*&%=!!!—

when my landlords' roofcow crashes
      the ceiling, dropping
         to my rose-flesh Persian. That scrying

carpet is my single possession
      with recherché réchaffé.
         Cow's name is Yazoo.

         She strikes

a perfect four-hoof landing
      like some estrogen-deprived Romanian, like
         Icarus with a back-up chute. After

her chutz-
    pah
         I can't manage to oompah

the money shot. I pull in my little satyr
    and hitch up my drawers
      and maybe sigh. Probably sigh.

Yes, I heave a sigh!
It's not every day that a cow kow-
tows

your orgasm. Is this a sign?
Is this the golden calf come home to roost?
Her brown eyes are *con dolorosa*

like

a Russian winter in one of those Czechered
novellas, those movies
turned film by tatting a soul

directly onto a negative.
Her orbs are honest brokers and as blue-
collar as jellied consommé

and they are judging me.
Am I blameworthy?
Am I on the wrong side of the cosmic

irony laws?
I have strayed
from the seven food groups.

Or are there five?
I do float in a cloud of general elysia.
Is this a crime? Am I trafficking malfeasia?

Yes—I am afraid of helpful insects—
ladybugs are spies, butterflies act
like they invented the wheel. And worms?

Well, parasites

are always *quothing* Sophocles—
    and I don't cycle or bicycle or recycle
        and do not tithe but I did filch

our neighbor's *People*. And once I set
    an orphanage on fire just to hear them babies
        scream.

Kidding! Egging you? Egging you on—?
    Is it that I never vote in elections yet I vociferously object
        to the elected?

        I do suffer from *autumnambulism*—

an acute strain of the doubting Tommies.
    I am the man who loses his faith in the home
        team the inning before

the great comeback.
    What's worse
        is that I adore the inning before

more
    than victory. I am a pitfall of chary.
        I dig the doom.

I'm like some vandal teen
    needling the Mahler Division
        in his black room. But it isn't just me.

These are dark days for our town.
    A virulent stain of self-schaden-
        freud-

        e

is replicating, spreading the boos.
        Not to mention the tangible poxes and plagues—
                rust festers our buds,

the winds have turned our apples tutti-frutti,
        the herds are skunked, our soaps
                are debunked, children are dead at birth,

or worse and our vaccines
        are defunct.
        The word curse

is bandied about; word & verse are candies
        for the devout.
                Athena

                        has put away her negligee.

Our king, Oedipus,
        sent his brother-in-law to Delphi
                to consult our oracle, Pythia.

These grim days have turned our citzs back
        to that ol' time relijun.
                When clouds sift black

                we shift our eyes to those that soliloquize.

Late last night I went to a bar
        to watch the oracle's variety show on HBO.
                She spoke in a voice between coo and woo:

                A rival will exploit a king's romance
                        with a lobbyist.
                Scientists will find dancing aliens
                        in a Mexican village.

Outlaw dolphins will meet in Texas
and swim to Disneyland.
A combat pilot will tell her husband
about her pay load.
A psychiatrist will help his ex
resurrect Neanderthal DNA.
A Chinese warlord will adopt
five English orphans.
Sexy rookie cops will search
for a serial killer on a porno set.

All the noddles at my groggery bobbed
to Pythia's non qua signs.
Any port in a storm, I guess.

Any storm in a port?

On the walk home I saw a stoning,
a book burning, an orgy,
and two and a half animal sacrifices

—BOW-OW-Ow-w.

Maybe Yazoo's nose-dive
into my hovel is a signal for me
to pause the calypso?

I can tell by the way her jaws tuffet my carpet
that she's an ungulate
with a plan. Once I had once been

ambitious.

In grade school I wanted to be
an astronaut slash
ballplayer. In high school I believed

rock god hash shop proprietor would be
    swell.
        In college I wore an orange Mohawk,

read post-neo-surrealist verse
    and dreamed
        of visiting Europe

on that trip-
    of-your-youth. Yeah,
        and with a sexy girlfriend who stayed

fresh and shaved even as we moto-biked
    over the Appian Way.
        Seventeen years later

I tire just reading the names
    of the new nations on the whey-
        colored atlas pages hiding the cracks

that hold up my walls. I am dim in places
    I can no longer see
        without EKGs.

My work?
    My vocation?
        My craft?

            My career?

I'm a professional queuer.
    That's right— is *that* clear?—I stand
        in lines. I wade

in time. I am the Duke
    of Earl in the state
        of wait. I worked for a major queuing concern.

I was assigned banks,
       pizza shops, and drug stores—
              prized clientele.

I studied lines and penciled reports
       that led to proposals on how to cut
              or gel hang-time according to their yen-

              zymes.

But our depression has made me obsolete—
       gulpable!
              Businesses are sucking Scyllapus ink.

Only the welfare line is pink.
       I read comics. I drink stink.

I rent a creep in this row house

in the Heckett, a spunkless district
       in sweet East Thebes, a hood
              of triple-deckers, worker cottages, cobras,

caverns, junkyards, derelict zoos, and dozens of taverns
       echo-located with the interdejection: O'.
              We are the maw

in mawkish. The kish, too.
       The abandoned research lab
              down my block left a working flock

of spider-sheep—they can mow your lawn
       and mend your sweater without one peop. Yes
              I'm haunted by charms.

I moved in after
       moving my father
              into the hospital. Rent was cheap. No

declension in the architecture
of faces facing last days long-
side me. This Thebes has the aura of after-

math—

after the parade, the demonstration,
the calculus, the rapture—always post
phoneme, spit and pyro.

What is so hypnotic
about suspended animation?
This is the Thebes that doesn't pretext.

When the shitake hit the fandango
we had already had our noses stuffed
with toga rags—ah—

As a singular hello—accept our soughs.
Only a diamond can cut
a diamond.

When you hear the black boots it's too late
for the palm reader.
Only a ghost can cut a ghost.

2

As Yaz grazes my heap of funnies
I consider what not to do.
A few are favorite pulps but I don't utter

word one.

I don't wish to alarm the beasties—
    the cow or my landlady
        Mrs. Pok. Mrs. Pok

is a blamer and I'm lined up,
    anew
        to wear the gnu flanks

and the Minotaur horns.
    When a claret-fueled home
        dyeing session tuned

her hair more pink than punk
    I was upbraided for unhinging
        the very fabric of time!

She claimed that me living over her living had tilted
    my floor
        (her ceiling)

and the paper-thin walls
    and her plywood shelves
        that held her only clock—making it unfeasible

for her to get a proper reckoning.
    I think her hair turned out nice,
        like ambulatory cotton candy.

When robot cleaners mauled
    her Pekinese,
        she declared that a radioactive leak

from my hotplate had reset
    her machines
        to mistake pup for fuzz.

Au contraire, Miss Astaire! I know!
    I rented a Geiger
        from Home Repo and checked—

and my rad-levels were below community standards—
    give
        or take.

She flirts with me, too, simply, because I'm
    Be-caused.
        Be-causèd?

I've seen photographs of Mrs. Betty Pok
    back when she was Betty Speck.
        Betty Speck looks

like
    the variety of young women who were
        going places.

In each photo her bright eyes sop
    you—this person from her
        future—and say:

Hello? Was there ever any question
    that I wouldn't become someone special?
        Then she was a sun that knew

        it was a star.

What turned her into the bossy nova?
    Living? Grace?
        Who toys with the man jerking off in your attic

unless you're pathetic?
    Maybe her flirting with I.M. Watt—(Me)—
        (the flagellate)—

is a form of self-flagellation?
    She lives like a whole note on a distaff
        of static.

She treats her husband
    like staff infection.
        That spouse, Pierre,

looks like a time-lapsed Christ—
    imagine
        Hey-Zeus riding his favorite ass

into Jerusalem then being cuffed
    and tried while being ex-
        coriated

ex
    post fact-
        to

by those blondeshells
    on *Court TV* and sentenced
        to 20 years hard time

for savior impersonation—that's Pete—
    a middle-aged Emanuel
        on work release.

Maybe that's why Mrs. Pok
    mocks Mr. Pok—he isn't right
        for our times—

where chattering teeth sack
    their pawns—
        where black choppers scatter like prawns.

3

        Back in my room:

Yaz's (Fy)odor is malevolent—
    it's enough to reanimate phantoms.
        Yet, why bitch?

The weather is dandy, blessing us
    in a passel of cancers. Leis
        of violet ash

light my bed. Doors are slamming
    which means doors
        were open! I'm snorting

sunshine.
    I hear chanting—football
        or gamy revival?

Something roly-holy.
    No surprise.
        Our district is a magnet

for believers.
    Its namesake, Clementine Heckett,
        founded a sect

who posted their big tops
    hereabouts.
        They were an argot cult

believing
    that the antique pantheon was literal,
       '   not Figaro. The Hecks favored

live death in their temples
    and slavery and ten holidays
      a month

with maenadic antics
    and dio-induced
      (diode-infused)

rapefests. But
    when the police caught Clem
      intimating with a toy poodle

he claimed was an afflicted nymph,
    his caboodle
      went to straight wrack and ruin.

      Crack and bruin?

A raven pokes her satin cowl
    through my gape
      and empties her beak.

Dear Sol, fleerful Apollo
    fades.
      I see

the thumbtacks that pin world to void.
    I hear cracking?
      Despackling?

Is this house ready to devolatilize
    me?
      The slate tiles

were swabbed for loam—
    good for roof cows,
        bad for roofs.

Our winter has had at the old wood.
    I know about dwarf cows.
        I know 57 or 58 things

about dwarfs. We had a herd,
    a kith
        on my grandparents' vineyard

near Ithaca,
    where my kin know a thing about journeys,
        we do.

We know about crops and bumper
    stickers and the moth effect
        of words.

I stomped 25 years
    with the grapes—
        with the leaf that doesn't turn.

All my days were tight as a tongue-
    d
        envelope.

All night under the aster fields,
    I waited for the umbilical
        trope

            to fall

like a magic rope, to con-
    strict
        like a bo-tree boa and heave me

to ma&pa.
        Mother left me with her folks, just
                months after my birth in New Haven.

She was a mask maker.
        Dad wrote plays.
                They were *artistic people*, Gramps said.

Our schism wasn't intended to wizen—
        to be forever. Soon as they settled
                I'd join up. Lickety-split—

that was the p/lot.
        I believe we all believed
                that someday they'd ripen and grow

to live
        with me. After
                someday came

and went that story
        went
                straight to fable.

As a boy, those weird cows came to my window
        to watch me
                play piano.

They lapped the pond as I lapped
        the pond. They gaoled
                my slap shots.

Grandfather taught me to throw
        the curveball—
                yukker, snake, deuce,

Uncle Charlie, Chief Bender, Roundhouse Lou—
    in a cow pasture.
        Tossing the cowhide

among the cows?
        Is that irony Socratic or bubonic?
            We were figurines out of yoke art.

Dwarf cows are not for main chow or college letter jackets.
    No
            they're designed to be

                a friend to man to whom thou say'st: moo.

My mother and me, my mother and I
    never had the chance
        to be more than pals.

Every month or three an envelope
    stuffed with drawings
        and photographs of them: at adventure.

I was her collector,
    she joked, she joked that her scraps
        would make me rich when she was

            a famous face-

maker. When I was 11 my mother,
    my mother
        dropped from a roof in L.A.

The police found her plop *troubling,*
    but ruled it death-by-misadventure-by im-
        port-

            unity.

The coroner clocked her blood-alcohol
        at 0.1927374.
                They found a bong

                        on the roof.

They were *artistic people.*
        Why, I asked,
                didn't she jump over Niagara Falls?

We could have watched
        from the Canadian side.
                Gran said: draw

a picture of your mother
        on a river.
                I drew five hundred; I scratched mother

onto windows of ice. I drew cows
        until the cows came home. *Now*
                who will collect me?

Weeks after she was buried,
        my father filled a van with her work—
                paintings, silver masks,

wire mobiles and stained glass,
        magic mirrors, CDs, modus,
                wax eyeballs and artist's books.

Her opus
        was hauled like trash
                and burned.

Gramps told me to draw cows.
        At least she never became
                a bitter pill.

Was that why she cashed her chips?
　　She saw gray waves and hitched
　　　　in the horse latitudes?

The pony platitudes? Ma
　　& Pa went west.
　　　　Just for a few years,

he told me,
　　just for a few bucks,
　　　　he told her

then we'll get Ike and get back, get back to our art.
　　He wrote satyr plays for TV.
　　　　She scanned soup cans

at the Soy Polloi, a market in Little Hanoi.
　　Next—she dropped from a roof.
　　　　The police found her

troubling.
　　Her death had a weak back-story.
　　　　Without a suicide

note or a rewrite
　　her story was forever raw.
　　　　Her death stippled

　　　　　　life.

My father hit the highways.
　　Every month or ten, I received a punch
　　　　in the solar plexus—

a postcard or grift:
　　a buffalo skull, wax teeth,
　　　　a Son House record.

He visited on holidays
    but no one no one ever asked—
        where the hell were you when my mother

           fell?

No one is a friendly ghost.
    The road led back to L.A.
        to work, which led to late night calls

to burn talk about me moving west.
    But habit would crapper
        his cropper—

a new project, a woman—the old rabbits—
    bitter pills and sad notes
        from the boo-hoo chorus.

He's the kind of dad
    who would have made a great uncle.
        He made me fear coming and going

           going and gone.

I learned to tread beer.
    I stayed in Ithaca.
        I took a few classes

at the colleges. I tended bar,
    held thick books, and played townie
        for a few years.

The year King Laïus was murdered
    my father moved to Thebes
        to seriously write seriously.

No more TV movies
    just T & A—
        tragedies and agonistes.

I visited.
    We drank.
        We locked

            horns.

We chased the same women.
    He was/is that rasher
        of father

who would have made a great brother.
    His plague arrived fast,
        fast

and hard
    —early onset Alzheimer's.
        Would you laugh

if I said I laughed?
    He was living with a young woman.
        Would you laugh if I said I cried?

At the end of her rope
    was my old man.
        I'm too young—she said—

some nights
    he can't remember who
        he has just fucked.

Join the club
    but
        I moved east to tap his slobber.

I was surprised
　　I went. I deserve no praise, see
　　　　see

I only came to assuage
　　the DNA
　　　　and buff the karmania.

　　　　　　Like him, like him I did it for me.

4

　　　　　　Back in my room:

from above I hear a squeak
　　should I moo
　　　　a warning to Yaz? Dwarf cows don't moo

they Mao
　　because their ululators combust at low
　　　　press. The cows were bioneered

so urbs could have fresh milk, laced
　　with graces—vitamins and serums
　　　　conveyed in compact, pet-like packages.

Even their shit is boutiqued.
　　It falls
　　　　in uniform pellets and smells like Zen.

On the farm, ours produced vein
　　blue milk with blood-clotting proteins.
　　　　We had one that created human

lacto globulins.
Landlady Pok is diabetic. Yazoo fashions
a quart of chocolate

insulinated milk per day.
Once I asked
a member of the labcoat gang
that came around our farm
on blue moons,
How do they do what they do?

He spent an hour with a sharp stick
scratching figures
in our dirt.

I saw I would never see.

Yazoo is the size of a sheepdog
with suction cup feet
like a goat.

She grazes on the golden grass
that grows off the loam-tiles.
She looks like a blue-eyed Mary

Mallon.
On hot nights when the moon
was stout

as sedation, I squeezed out
my crescent window and shimmied
up the tin rainspout

to join Yazoo.
In case of rain there's a lean-to
constructed from broken umbrellas.

From the peak
    you can peek
        at the sloops in the harbor.

I'd bring up one book for reading
    and one book
        for feeding.

Yaz likes poetry—
    above all she licks the classics—
        she sics rhyme to her fiber.

We made it through all of Donne's
    Holy Sonnets in one night. As I read:
        "I am a little world made cunningly…"

she was already making cud:
    "Or wash thee
        in Christ's blood,

which hath this might
    that being red, it dyes red souls
        to white."

Yaz finishes my comics and loosens
    an ololuge
        as sad as a squeeze toy in a childless house.

She looks ready to descend
    to the main course.
        Her stomachs are churning.

But the door
    from the attic
        to the staircase

is locked from the outside.
The Poks prefer
that I take the fire escape

for entry and exit.
I'm about to explain this to Yaz
when she kicks in the door

with her back legs. Next,
she Sherpads
down the dusty flights at yikes-speed.

When I don't hear screams
I follow and find Mrs. Pok
sitting on a tatami mat.

The TV is playing
a news debate program.
Their machine is a 144-inch Narcissus.

On the screen skin-covered skulls
are at opposite sides of a severe
wooden table. Their mouths plow

like whales raking krill. Their faces
are gut issue red like a dreadnaught's
wattle.

Tizzy snot flies from their nostrils,
spit distends like
vanilla taffy from their lips—epiglottis

waggle like

white worms
off distich hooks.
The station crawl hawks

male penile implants and tracks
    the pundits' blood pressure
        and pulse hate.

          Electroencephalographic
leads
    taped to their hairless pates look like deep-
      sea tentacles. They're debating
our current crisis.
    One is for the Oedipus
      one is against
the king.
    One digs Pythia
      one is versus
the oracle.
    One admires Creon,
      but one is in animus of all royals.
One is with Apollo—
    one is with Dionysius.
      I can't see
Yaz but Mrs. Pok
    is purging into a silk dirge rag
      while gazing
into a hand mirror.
    Their furniture is bichromatic—
      pink and green
and plastic.
    Wake talc blots the air.
      "Mrs. Pok? Sorry but—"

"Isaac Watt! What does *he* want from *me*? Why won't *he*
negotiate *his* own devils? *We* all have our ills and our bills.
You know *he's* still practicing Xmas? Says *he* loves the bells
and the elves. We'll be in laughingstocks."

She threads her pronouns like epithets.
Surgery has mimped her lips
so that her words sound like asides.

Her lids are tinted agape blue.
Her pupils are black checkers, like
Orphan Annie

meets Mister Benzedrine.
She wears a gray sack dress
with asparagus leggings.

Her hair is bowl-cut
with a greased shark fin
on top—like a kid in fopzine.

I don't understand what she means
so I nod.
Yes. OK.

Some days the message-in-the-bottle
is the medium
of exchange.

"What do you see when you see this?"

She closes one eye and rubs
her hand against her forehead,
her tongue grubs

from the side of her mouth.
I listen for Yaz.

My nose is no help, as the room

is being spritzed with Rain-
After-Sex-
With-A-Masked-Stranger,

a top-ten odor this year. I prefer
Reproach-the-Uncharitable-Man,
but

that's me—
Mr. Sent-
imental.

"Isaac Watt? Are you looking?"

She presses her palms into her cheeks.
I fear her brain will leak
from her head like zit lava.

"Edvard Munch? *The Scream*?"
From the kitchen, I hear the chirr
of a chewing bovine.

I walk toward Pok
to peek around the corner
at Yaz, nosing

breakfast, repealing
Mrs. Pok's banana slippers.
"What are you doing?

I mean, with your funny-funny faces?"
I say
to distract Pok from cow.

"I'm preparing for the worst, Isaac. I'm high on know-how as
    you know from our visitations, when you pass rent through
    the mail slot. I study the crime television dramas and the
    shows on forensic science. I like to read pamphlets on body
    disposal and fingerprint degradation. Do you know what it
    is when I say—forensic science?"

"No," I say, "I guess
    I don't."
        Sometimes you have to let thunder have its rain.

"Forensic science is the debate that occurs when corpses appear.
    These programs feature people who know their way around
    a chewed bone or exit wounds. I've found the number one
    explanation that people are convicted of murder in this, our
    nation our city. Do you know this reason?"

"That they've killed
    someone?"
        Mrs. Pok considers my answer.

"*That* may be but *that* is beside my point. My pet reason that
    people are *convicted* of murder is that the *jury* believes they
    look guilty. Persona! My peers say, 'they showed no emotion'
    or 'they looked shifty.' If that's true, Isaac, then that's the
    truth."

On the tube
    a pundit demands that Oedipus
        find the man who witnessed

Laïus' murder.
    He uses the word
        cover-up.

"I don't know about you, but I don't plan on spending my Golden
   Fleece years in prison orange. What if my Pierre were to
   meet with gruesome ends? Just think of the reckless way
   that man gardens. And what if *while* the police were
   conducting their case into Pierre's kippered head or his
   lawn-mown belly they noted that *me, his wife* and their
   a-cutest suspect was not carrying on? What if I can't wail
   on cue, Isaac? What if inside that wood-paneled court of
   law I don't wrench my panic into: stricken victim?"

Her eyes change from blue to black.
   She smiles.
      Her eyes flood

as the cow hops
   to the floor to begin
      in on a stack of lo-carb cookbooks.

"Why I'll be!" Mrs. P says as she sees Yazoo.

Her voice is putty.
   This is probably the closest
      she has ever been to a cow.

Dumbots do the milking and deliver
   the product to the Poks' front door
      in glassine Baggies.

"Is this why Pierre sent you in here, Isaac? Don't lie for that
   lump of coal. Actually she's cute. Housebroken? She is a
   she?"

Mrs. Pok looks stoned
   and happy.
      We might get out of this yet.

"Isaac, speaking of killing Pierre, that hospital phoned about your
   father. Or is your father your mother?"

"What
      was the
          message?"

"I remember that? They called days ago. You can't expect me
   to remember that far back. Days ago? Or is your brother
   your father? That's it. Does it eat?"

It was strange for the Patchen Industries Hospital
   to phone. My father
      is part of a trial

procedure, to cure his Alzy's. Patchen
   doesn't need
      my money.

                    I've looped the loop.

5

Mrs. Pok lets me use her cell
      which is shaped like a fuzzy die and hangs
          off her neck. The hospital voice

won't release Dad's specs. The voice
      is without perspiration.
          Computer or constipation?

That would be rude
      to ask
          and imprudent to chance.

"You needed to be here yesterday. See Dr. Kac, pronounced cats."

I excuse myself from Pok and pet,
and ascend to my room to change
into my dad-visiting duds. There's a slab
of gumwood and two wine crates
that I use as a desk.
Sometimes I sit there and draw

my unlit room. I write letters
I never mail.
I sit with my hands lapped
and my eyes shut
and imagine a white sun melting
a white fog.

When he called Ithaca, he laid it out—
his health:
failing
and "his lady"
had exited, stage right
and he couldn't afford
a nurse and he wasn't ready
for a home.
"No shit, Sherlock,"
I said and he said,
he wasn't ready
to die—alone—
would I join him?
He made it sound
like a vacation—an adventure—

his gift.
    I close my eyes and wonder
        why my life

is like watching English
    subtitles
        to an English-language movie.

In a corner a spider tacks her net.
    Above the makeshift desk,
        on the wall,

is a photo of Dad and me
    on the world's smallest
        suspension bridge.

We each have a foot on one shore.
    He's making devil horns
        behind my head.

"It's your duty," my Gran said.
    "You're over 30, kid,"
        Gramps said,

"take a chance—you'll never make it as a farmer.
    You don't have the thumbs
        for vines."

When I first came to Thebes
    we lived in the Kevlar District,
        in a low-rise

overlooking
    Dragon Park.
        The four rooms were filled

with the detritus of my father's travels,
more junk than antique.
Now and then,

a check would come, residual
from a low-brow
he had worked on.

He got up each day
and pretended to write
but we made it

only from what I could scrounge.
My 24 college credits
qualified me

to fill out employment forms.
I wanted to hate my father.
I want to hate my father.

When I arrived
I was ready to pick a dozen fights
over a hundred scores.

But
he was rounding the bend.
Alzheimer's—

the man wasn't 60.

His state was enough to send lightning
down your spine.
What God did he forget to blow?

Mornings we might talk
but by evening he had forgotten
me—houseboy?

Driver? Agent
of the irregular
regulators?

Once I played along
and interrogated him
until

he gave me up.

We became too much to handle.
There was no nest egg
to scramble.

So I sent him out
for service.
I found Dad a spot in a cheap hospice.

The people were sweet,
even if their methods
were backwards—

rhubarb enemas and grasshopper
gene therapy.
It was all I could afford.

Then a doctor came from the Patchen.
He said
your pater is the perfect fodder

for radical treatment. He said that a backer
was prepared to procure
our ills—sign here.

His red head was Chiaed
with hair plugs—pre-Hydra,
like each tuft was a serpent

hatchling.

Sign here and here and here.
    We're using cutting-edge science!
      He said

maybe—cross your fingers and hope
    not to die—I might have a father
      back, with time.

        Sign here, here, and there and here.

All I wanted was a father
    to hate and punch and defenestrate
      like all the other kids?

I Jeffersoned the Hancock line. I moved to the Heckett, where
    I stare at the wall
      and it stares back.

Walls!
    Can't live with them:
      can burn them to ash.

6

Outside, I find Mr. Pok
    on his hands-and-knees planting
      in the 10 x 10 foot postage stamp

he calls a front yard.
    A paper warbler sings
      from the tin gutter

which amplifies the bird's bark
    into a sonatina.
      Did the bird discover this knack

on her own? I sigh
   to get Mr. Pok's attention.
          Our house is across the street

from a veteran's hostel—a nerve-
   red brick square,
          nearly

a million years old. True! Built
   as a schoolhouse
          then converted

into a prison, then a factory, next
   a depository
          and finally, now

it serves as all four.
   The patients are
          free to come and skedaddle

but they mainly
   stay put
          as put shots.

When the weather allows they sit
   in the front yard
          in flimsy wickers.

They smoke home-rolled,
   drink
          brown-bagged liquor, wave

at passing cars, play canasta
   and listen to planted
          music-buds.

A few tend the rose bushes
    that grow
        along the side of the building.

They wear Victorian gardening clothes
    and use shears as stern
        as mandibles.

The younger ones, ones my age,
    the survivors
        of the economical truth campaigns

sport animatronic limbs
    and blue skin
        that salves radiation poisoning.

I guess
    there's hope
        that dope might be darned

that develops their urge
    —développé? —
        to go somewhere—like

back to war,
    back to work, like
        back to war.

        "Bulbs?" I ask my landlord.

"No, Isaac, no. Look at you—you're dressed sharp as a pine
needle. On important business? Sweet. Bulbs? No, Isaac.
I have enough ideas. Get it? In cartoons light bulbs stand
for ideas? Light implies light?"

"That's funny," I say, shuffling for an exit
strategy.
He removes a greeting card
from his seed bag. Pierre's face is streaked
with grizzle.
He piles his hair
into a pompadour threatening to convert
into a bouffant.
His Fu Manchu looks
foo infused.
But, he's a good man.
He speaks to me even when
he doesn't want a thing. He doesn't want a thing.
"What's this?
You're burying old cards?
Recycling are we, Pierre?"
"New cards, Isaac. Christmas cards, music cards, listen to this."
He opens it up and I hear
a children's funereal choir singing along
to an analog Moog:
Hark how the bells,
sweet silver bells,
all seem to say throw cares away...
"What's with the humbug, sir?
Santa leave you a lump of coal
last Christmas?"

"Coal? Let me think," he says, handing me a card. On the front
is a cartoon bird. In the word bubble it reads: TWEET
JESUS LOVES YOU. "I don't recall receiving lumps."

"Interring the evidence?
    Worried about the police?"
        He smiles like a fondue skewer, on the skew.

"It's moles, Isaac! The whole district is infested with moles, and
the worst kind, too, the clever fellows that chew your
vitals—gas, electric, sewer—and then they taproot your
phone and hide in your wooden horses and hitch into your
Internet and mind your sweet lovemaking.

"Isaac, I unearthed tunnels from tomatoes to cukes, from my
Indian moons to my Mexican sour Gherkins!

"It's not in me to kill them, outright—but this is war! When the
moles hear these Xmas carols they think they're not alone!
Scares the hells out of them and off they go to hollow some
pagan's garden. They can't stand to hear the good news."

I nod and let the gentle man
    return to his war.
        I point my nose north and smell

            the hospital text.

7

I keep to the poplar-lined avenue,
    following the blemished streetcars
        through a channel between Main and Pegasus

where old sedans smolder
like goose bumps on the gooseflesh
of eye-jobs—witnesses

to the footstep, the fingerprint, the going rate.
I slam the gates behind me
and take the short-cut

through Thebes Greens.
I'm a buck, a pink bud blowing
through a faun's defunct wood.

I need one drink; just one
blink
and then I'll visit dear old Dad.

The moon bug-juices the vistas
between the trees
and unseals

a succession of events, past and future.
A carbide lamp embedded in the sky reveals
children, stained

like live cells—
a street gang in a cemetery wearing wire
coat hangers on their heads

like antlers or antennae—
I can't tell
by their curds and sine waves whether

they are deer or aliens.
Stags or Mars-kins?
Dad wrote a bit about Selene,

the moon goddess. In the classic version
    she falls head hard for Endymion,
        the shepherd.

Each night
    she metaphors him
        to sleep. Selene begs Zeus

to grant Endy
    eternal life. In Dad's take
        he wants a movie deal,

with points. In either case, Zeus agrees
    and places him in perpetual perchance,
        so that each night

Selene can visit E
    in her temple, in Asia Minor.
        (In Japanese the L and R

are interchangeable rates,
    so in anime you have
        Serene).

Through the trees the children's faces blush
    like selenium under rice paper.
        Clouds push back and I stagger on.

The path follows the willow-lined
    river, north,
        following

famished catamarans through the shoals,
    and a shoal
        of yachts that dock

at the Grand Hotel.
    Savory music from the lounge
        makes my toes tap. I imagine, like in a Tex

Avery cartoon
    that X-
        ray machines are wheeled into the lobby

and used to see through
    Florsheims and Ferrettis
        and black silk stockings

to see phalanges tapping. This is the place
    for me—
        out of my league—

out on the ledge.
    It's a family fracture,
        like our pumpkin heads

            like our jack-o-lantern teeth.

The hotel's gateway keeper—as warm
    as a facula—hotspurs me
        into Magog's Bar and Grill.

The room is as tight as mofo dojo.
    On the stage, behind a bharal shoji,
        is the band—

The Ethylenes—
    a shofar, plastic bucket, and theremin
        trio—

see no light at the end of our short tunnel.
    No, siree.
        They play that robin's-egg blues.

This is the home of the compulsory
        jazz scene. I join the sack-
                heads

at the ash blonde counter, filling-up
        on koi colored liquids.
                In my mind's TiVo that cartoon

is still rolling, without
        res or resh or res-
                ervations but now that imaginary X-

ray gizmo—
        a flat-screened TV with feet—
                is manned

by a gadgeteer, a gadfly who offers
        peeks
                inside skulls at one buck a pop.

A dollar for a dollop of cranium uranium.
        One hundred cents
                for one exacto

swathe of sense. I check my pocket
        for change—nope, yep—nothing
                but shells.

On the TV above the counter, a deft-
        boned wonky is reporting
                that Teiresias, the soothsayer,

the K Street player, the con-
        mystic from Mystic, Conn,
                is being culled from the Palace.

I look down on the counter and conject:
What gawds swarm inside these
bawdish beans?

Am I one of these?
I'm already a little drunk, a heck
half-seas

over, sure but the beer is beer
and the music
is in close proximity to music.

Teiresias sports
two
apple green monocles.

A woman wearing a Glengarry and spectacles
made from Vaseline glass
takes the saucer

next to mine. She throws a few sous
across the Suntory-stained countertop.
That sou-sou hisses

like frost on a blossom,
like stars in a casino fountain. Like plovers?
Like plovers?

Like Egyptian plovers standing in Nile ale?
I can't see that.
I try to boo her limbus to etch through

her spyglass.
I think about proposing
some statements

for her to agree or disagree with, using
   the Likert scale like at work, like:
      "Sound and Vision"

is the quintessential 21st C. drawing room minuet,
   or:
      Things were gooder and older

in the good ol' days, or:
   The uncouthwashed
      must have their heads severed!

The woman swirls her Glenlivet
   until the whiskey illuminates her face
      in a brunette spot.

The band segues into that chestnut,
   "We'll Always Have Vesuvius,"
      as she pulls

her silver microphone
   from her silver lamé handbag,
      and begins to sing: Woe to us, baby,

and when she sings I know
   that she is the singer.
      I'm clever, clever like that.

But really, a runer who croons
   from her stool?
      Who knew? I know

she is the singer Sam Phillips
   called for. Euripides
      called our custom a Phrygian one.

Put a security blanket on her,
    says one of the de menthe drinking mooks
        stationed at the bar.

By this he means Linus—
        the de Laurentisian personification
            of song

of lamentation, the agent
        of the tender life
            of vegetables, destroyed

by the fiery heat of Sirius
        the beagle-star. Imp-pressed,
            I am.

                Woe to us.

Before the quicksand covers my Zeno,
    I quit
        and light for the bathroom.

My feet slide over the parquet
        like a Brinker on Percodan
            skating athwart

a ballroom reclaimed
        from the North Sea.
            Who is that woman—?—

that singer—that myth-
        antrope
            who stresses the beat

of my heart?
        The bathroom is as opulent as a copulant's
            opuntia

at a Prince Creon orgia or so I hear,
    or so they say,
        in *The Theban Rag.*

The tiles are a poor Corinthian's
    leather, the walls
        are made from narwhal tusk

and engraved with grand scenes
    from our Theban mystery—
        dragon teeth, the seven gates of Kadmos,

the abduction of Europa,
    the sown-men,
        the Thebes Sox loss to East Argos.

Each toilet seat
    is hand-carved from Carreran marble.
        How do I know this?

It's all in the edifying brochure
    I'm given at the door
        (cross-hatched

in redwood hatched by Vulcan hisself).
    Attendants offer me a musk spritz,
        a shoeshine, hot towels and shots

of absinthe (gulp) or was that aftershave?
    Through teak Finnish speakers
        I hear her who makes my knees free-range spaghetti.

I imagine her bellybutton sprouting sunflowers
    and her hair (gold, red,
        or is it sable?) enclosing me

in a hirsute cage.
      I ask an attendant
            to slap me sane, but the price for that service

is out of my range.
      I walk into a free stall
            and see a plaque above the throne:

                  Oedipus Shat Here.

Wow—you don't say! It's my day!
      I take a seat and check my leaflet
            for more essentials.

On the cover is our king
      before he was our king.
            It portrays a faux-hawked Oedipus,

in a blood-soaked toga wrapped once
      in a red stripe across his torso
            into which

the Sphinx, that craven minx,
      has sunken her fore-claws.
            Her brunt paws

objectify his groin and her bare breasts
      are pressed, definitively,
            into his roiled chest.

Fledged wings extend
      from her shoulder blades
            several feet above her head.

She and Oed peer
      a-
            cutely

                  penetratingly into each other's eyes.

Her cat-o'-nine
    is coiled like cobra, ready to Batusi.
        Oedipus's head is bent

downward, un-in-
    timidated—
        like he's me here on the head

(imagine—my rank-and-file
    dejecta
        is larking about with royal ooze).

He's about to answer her quiz
    and bail out Thebes
        from our earlier pesters.

His feet are bootless, but fester
    no sign
        of the famous injury

(infamous perjury—? —
    campaign perfumery?)
        which gave him his get, his nick, his handle—

        Oedipus—meaning *ye olde swell-*

fella
    The singer segues into the standard,
    "Scat Scan":

        On the road to Delphi
            you meet a lot of shoe-flies
        On the way to Shanghai
            you best avoid the cat's eye
        On the trail to Dubai
            you can watch your skin fry

On the path to Versailles
            you hear that haunted hi-fi
    and she sings…
            like this—
    Burn, burn, burn
            let's scat 'til the end

                    'til the end of time

According to our secret police
        after Oedipus
            answered her riddle

the Sphinx plummeted
    from our city wall.
            She leaped to her death.

They fall in bunches, these women.
    But I'm the one declining.
        I feel dizzy, oh-so dizzy.

Is it what I ate? Drank? Stank? Or is it
    something I touched like chaos
        (or (ahem) Kaos?)

or a cow, dissolution, and viscous gloom?
    I'm spinning like a fun-house room.
        I close my eyes, and chew on her song.

When I was seven, the DNA units
    came to Ithaca to visit, to allay
        their batteries. Dad took me to Syracuse

to watch the Orangemen play
    the Spartans.
        Mom let me assist

with a set of masks she was making
for a production
of *J'accuse*…!

I painted mine red with white spots.
She said it was lovely,
but not right for her show, she said,

"Your mask is too special, the crowd won't be able to hear the
words. The best mask is the one the mob forgets."

"I could never make it as a mask maker, eh, Isaac?"

I return from my knock-
out
to a woman's articulation

from the other side
of my stall door—a voice
from across the strange particulate.

"Knuckle-knuckle! Let me in or I'll huff the short hairs of your
thingy thing-thing!"

Are these deluxe poopers co-ed?
I apologize
and pull up my pants.

When I open the door—
there she is—the singer—
but you *know* that. *Knew* that?

But do you know I don't know where
we're at?
I emerge

from a portable potty to find us outdoors.
    The air is cold: the night
        is night:

the moon
    looks like that sour mouth that says, *Shutup*—
        before you even get a chance to speak.

"Speak Isaac—kine got your tongue?"

And even though she looks
    nothing like the creature
        on the brochure I know it's her.

She transmits,
    she Warhols her ID
        to my soul.

            "You're the Sphinx."

"Riddle me this, Isaac Makepeace Watt—oh just kidding! Stop
    trembling. There's plenty of time for shaking and baking you
    in an oven, later."

No tail,
    no talons,
        no wings, I think, and she says,

"Don't be so sure of that. The best mask is one the mob forgets."

I can smell sewage and cotton candy.
    I place where I am—
        Pluto Park.

Behind us
    is the ornamental band shell
        and the Memorial

to the Victims of the Great Tragedy.
    On the river
        mist tumbles like baled lambkins.

On the river
    a decommissioned military amphibious vehicle
        totes supplicants.

They honk like ducks.
    The Sphinx beeps back.
        The Memorial to the Victims

of the Great Tragedy is:
    two rows of 13 subway kiosks.
        There is one

entrance for each letter.
    Children are often brought here
        to learn their alphabet.

The visitor first chooses a station
    usually the letter
        for a relative or loved one

or for a stranger
    on their Victim's Aid Bracelet
        and then they turnstile

and walk down the 72 steps.
    Obviously
        the number

is symbolic. Children
    are brought here to learn
        to count to 72.

The visitor then waits
for their train to arrive.
As they pass they linger.

Some read the colorful literature;
some appreciate the bandito graffito.
Many pray or cry.

Once on board they sit
in the comfortable seats and listen
to patriotic airs while

the conductor calls out
the names:
"Aaron Michele, Aaron Nathaniel, Aaron Oren…."

The train doesn't really move.
It rocks and trembles— specious FX.
The view out the windows is blank.

But some claim to see things like:
an intense electric light or a flash
of mist that takes a shape and of course, some

see their dead.

My first visit underground was when
I was in grades. My grandparents
took me. I wore

the bracelet for a Mary Steed.
We waited in a line as long
as an elephant's nose or so the song goes.

A bearded man eating candy apples
protested the Xs
and the Zs, which he called zeds.

"It wasn't fair," he said, "that unpopular letters receive their own train."

When we were under I looked out the window
    and saw a woman
        in a white shift.

I knew it was Mary
    but didn't whisper a word—
        until now. Until you.

"Excuse me, sir and/or ma'am?"

We turn to find pilgrims—
    a man,
        a woman and a child.

"Mind if you take our picture? Over in front of the Memorial?"

"No," says the Sphinx. "I'd be delighted. Is there a particular
    station you want to stand below?"

The adults shake their heads.
    The child's red hair
        is divided into two uneven braids.

The Sphinx flicks her split tongue
    at the kid, filling her animal soul
        with brat's milk.

The woman looks at the river.
    The man stares at his hands.
        After she snaps their photo they offer

to return the favor. The Sphinx
    declines and looks up, fast, jabbing the air
        with a black fingernail.

"What?" I ask
     seconds before the sky reverbs
       with adjectives from a squadron of fighters.

"Prince Creon's private air force—something Danish has hit the fan."

When I turn
     from the planes I don't see
       the family.

"Jesus! Such a simple question," the Sphinx says licking her
     bleached teeth. "All they had to do was choose a letter."

She takes a step
     toward me. I can taste her pelt on my lips.
       I'm going to die—I know it—

          But why?

"Even Buddha left his tent, on the sly—to shit. Why Ike? Why
     not? Thanks to the politicos' polity there's a plague a-
     seizing. And each Theban gets the diseasing—they deserve.
     You warrant a stiff question."

The trees begin to rustle, or laugh.
     She rubs her knee against my knee.
       She weaves

her fingers through my fingers.
     She chests me
       into a kiosk wall.

"Isaac, why do birds suddenly emerge every time I'm on the
     verge?"

Huh? That's it? —must be a trick question.
     She hums
       the theme song from *Jeopardy*.

A citizen runs past us, yelling: "Queen Iocasté is out with the
　　ebb! She's slipped her cable! She's crowbait, relic,
　　reliquiae! Her *corpus* is *delecti*! Oh, our Queen, Iocasté
　　sings in the invisible choir! She's crossing on the Stygian
　　ferry! She's giving an obulus to Charon! The Queen is at
　　the end of her beaded rope! She's pushing up Prussian
　　daisies; she's given up the ghost! She's worm kibble!"

"Just like moi
　　　they long to qua—
　　　　　close to you?" I sing.

The Sphinx pushes away from me, spitting: "Oh—you cursored
　　brat! I'm dissolving! Melting! I'm turning soft-core!
　　Oh—what an orb—what a sphere!"

Now she'll have to hurl herself
　　　off a wall.
　　　　　Or melt? I'd like to see that?

"Neither, goof-off-ocles" she says. "Isaac, you believe all the
　　proper ga-ga you're fed. But, you do win a lovely parting gift
　　for your troubles. Pucker up."

So I do.
　　　And she punches my face:
　　　　　$@#*&%=!!!—

8

I open my eyes to sunlight,
　　　and fasten them, tight—I speak
　　　　　but... very... words ache

verily.
 I hear voices:
  mumblers, mutterers, musths and several burblers.

I unsnap my oglers and find
 I'm in a park? Another park?
  Then, through the metaphors I see a sign:

The Patchen Industries Hospital.
 Not only did the Sphinx let me live,
  she put my place in me.

The morning is famous.
 The autumn sun is on parole
  from its jam-jar.

The hospital is wedding gown white cake
 made by Swiss Re.
  I wouldn't be surprised if it saucered

and warped and woofed home to Phobos—
 the residents are elderly:
  infixed. Men

women
 who no longer play q's and a's.
  They won't tie your shoes.

Their faces are stained
 with halfway-house moue. Their people
  have exchanged their bodies

for holding beds. And hope, yep, sure
 a millidrop of hope. In an oak tree
  is a brown star flitter,

a bird-
    like chimera made from space-tin
      and no bigger than my fist.   .

The yellow in its coverts
    makes its wings appear serrated,
      like they might be calculated

to sever a head or two.
    Past the speechifiers,
      other 86'd walk a figure-8-path.

The lawn is sheared to a country club trim.
    There are Kithairon laurels and dwarf scab shrubs.
    Black heart bushes

describe the path's edge.
    Fat berries litter
      the ground and their dark juice stains

the coral cement.
    Some patients wobble, some
      move like protractors. Some

are able to perambulate
    on their own while others
      have robots shaped like turtle shells

rigged to their spines.
    One of the men notices
      me

and says, "Can I come with you to Hell? There are still things I
    can do well."

I mosey into the shade
of an apricot tree.
I am divisible.

"Isaac Watt?" asks the star-flitter.

This is a day for firsts. I've never
conversed
with a metal bird.

I'm nervous, like
when a probe-wielding doctor
alienates one's innateables.

"Dr. Kac will see you now."

"Thanks,
Sir and or
Ma'am?"

Inside, the décor is static.
I'm an extra in a satyr-e
based on English TV. Tapestries

of boar hunts hang
from cinnabar (not red!) walls.
The furniture is dark and Cimmerian—

my back aches from the glaring.
The marble floors make my heels
sound important.

"Isaac, in," says Dr. Kac.

He sits behind a pier table
made of glass. His lab coat is yellow.
"What's wrong with my father, Dr. Kac?"

He raises his arms into...
     surrender?
     Touchdown?

"You said my real name! Will I metamorph into a pillar of salt?
     Most say cack or cass or even, and this will surprise you
     smart smart fellow, even they say kazz. The forming of the
     words with the letters in a conventionally accepted order
     throws off the pronouncing. The lip-smacking. 'I am the
     shell that migrates in reverse, from strand through waves
     and into the sea!' What is wrong with your native mouths?"

His voice carries the low-honk
     of the Great Lakes wedded
          to a vowel-less Eurapital.

He laugh-tracks and snaps his salsa
     and pepper ponytail
          through the ionized air.

"Please, take a seat younger Watt. See the tube?" He points at a
     flat screen in a gilded frame. "They're now saying the King
     and the Queen *are* brother and sister. *Were?* Do you
     believe that gingerbread crumble? We are watching the
     world as smut film. Funny. Droll. Witty. Comic. But sad,
     too. Gloomy. Cheerless. Heartbreaking. Like a deveining?
     These royals! Their orbits have high eccentricity—they
     deviate from our perfect circle. This suggests that they
     did not originate in cultural acquisition. Their sins may
     be contagious. You feel a fever coming on? You are your
     father's fruit? Do you pee close to his tree? I watch his
     movies—the bad ones, the plays he wrote? Yes?"

On TV a reporter stands with a chorus
of reporters
on the palace steps.

It seems only yesterday
that that way was strewn with believers
pleading for Oedipus to help.

"I've seen a few," I say.
"Dr. Kac
is his condition worse?"

He opens the kind of book called a tome. He uses his finger to
find the verse. "Visit, often, do you? Rhetorical. Your father
has been ours for seven months. You've only visited—ah—
zero times? How will that rap sheet appear spread over the
court of law?"

On TV, a helicopter shot: the royal kids—
Antigonê, Ismenê, Eteoclês, and Polyneicês—
are being led

out the back door with hoods
on their heads,
like little asps being taken back to the jungle.

"Well, I don't lick your shoes. I won't judge. We have judges to
adjudicate. Must be a bitch when your old man doesn't
remember teaching you to pitch a ball or how to ball. What
do you do, son? In Thebes? For living?"

"I wait.
I wait
in lines."

"Of course you do! Not the farm life, huh? I wouldn't want
to know how many hours a week I wait. But, what's your

occupation? Job? Do you say career? That would be
interesting you *saying* career. Do? Give it a try? Say, 'My
career is fill-in-the-blank.'"

On TV Creon's jets shoot
    down
        the TV whirlybirds.

The chorus of journalists sways back and forth in lament.
On TV
        soldiers are leading Pythia,

that blistered seer,
    on a perp walk.
        Kac flips the picture to MTV3:

The Ethylenes and the Sphinx,
        playing at Cafe Largo.
            She turns to camera three and blows

                me a kiss.

"Oh yes, Isaac, your father—is William Watt?"

"Y

    e

        s."

"Dead, alas. Simple heart failure. Your Billy Watt died yesterday."

"I'm glad
    it was
        simple."

"Good, good the dark humor will grease your melancholia. Do
    you know what we do here, Isaac? Guess on, lover—
    going to blow your mind what we do. You'll think you're
    starring in a sciencefictionary."

On TV, they cut away
    from videos
        to that hot reality show, *Peripeteia*.

"No guess? Well, in a nutshell, we have the ability, Isaac, the
    numbers and equations, to move, to shift, to groove and lift
    the memories stowed in the human brain into another
    brain. We gene memes! Like downloading? Like
    lowdowning! Memories your father can't raise or rewire are
    patterned then acquired using our amazing top-secret know-
    how thingamajiggery."

"You moved
    my father's memories
        into another patient's brain?"

"No, that's diabolical, Isaac. That's ma-cob-bray. No, what do you
    take us for? We moved the memories of your father into
    the brain of a mountain gorilla. It works better with gorillas.
    I'll be honest—we don't know why. Our gasts are flabbered.
    Homo sapien to primate—that's the golden ticket."

"I see," I lie.
    I knew there was talk
        about doing these things—

I read about it
    in the newspapers,
        I saw the protests—

but you never imagine that they'll do this
    to your own
        monkey.

"So you *see* but you look sad without the ha-ha? Why? This isn't
    all a rainy Monday. Your father is dead. But the gorilla? The
    gorilla is not dead. You can visit the gorilla, today. Before the

gorilla's brain is, how *you* put it, downloaded into a new site."

"Where?
Downloaded
where?"

"Don't know, Isaac. I'm a doctor of money! You know? In the phenyl group? Economist, investment tanker, entrepreneur. The money is mine, the science is theirs, I mean the brains are minds, but also theirs. Also mine? Sorry—too many 'ohs' to track! Plus, did I mention that you signed the contract in red ink—you did. But that's the bridge underwater—go, now. Enjoy a fond tata to your Papa. This is a rare chance—*rara hertz*. See we are not malefactors! Isaac, check the contract—it will erectify in any court, in any land! We're not the bad guys. We didn't invent death and disease. Lucky you, Isaac Watt, who waits in lines. Marvelous! This world?"

9

After my meeting with Kac,
    the star-flitter
        leads me to the pool, to the gorilla.

The birdbot explains
    the schematics, the science
        behind the lather, but all the b-

        lather

about: neuron loss—
    patterned temporal lobes—
        implicit learning—

other-wiring—meat
 algorithms—protein therapy agents—
  personality diffusion—

courses of therapy—
 parallel dimensions—
  automata viruses—

acetylcholine restoration—
 synthetic biology—and neuron
  synapses: leaves me wobbly.

It says that the gorilla
 is fitted with a voice generator,
  near its larynx.

   It will speak to me.

"Can't my father's memories
 be copied
  into something else?

Like into you—a robot,
 or a hard-drive?
  How about a clock radio?"

"Possible," says the tin bird, "but illegal. Like incest.."

The hallways are empty.
 The high windows smother the sunlight.
  "What can I expect from the ape?"

"The gorilla mixes his own life with your father's life and with
 TV and movies and books. The gorilla has a polyglot reality.
 It's difficult to know where one mind ends and the other
 begins. Even in the secular sense. Even in the same
 sentence. That's the trouble with human processors.

They're caught up in their words. And words invoke such
marrow attachments, that your outputs often miss the
world."

Tweet Jesus.
    The robot leaves me at a steel door.
        The heart

is a bird cured of flight.
    Inside, I find the gorilla
        sitting on the lip

of a lap pool. He wears
    khaki clam diggers.
        His bare feet churn

the ministering waters.
    He has white patches
        around his ears.

Under a straw hat is a large head
    with a broad, flattened nose.
        His nostrils flare.

His arms are as long as my legs,
    his eyes are like wasp paper
        in November, nest abandoned.

What do I say? Can I live
    below
        the by-line?

"My genitals are small, relative to overall body size."

The gorilla's voice sounds like Charles Laughton
    in *Island of Lost Souls*—opulent
        and loco-motive

with blood and starch.
    He bares his yellow teeth
        and arches an eyebrow.

I smell beer.
    "How's the water?
        Warm?"

"Apart from humans, gorillas have few or no predators."

"I'm not
    a predator—I'm your son. Isaac.
        I promise."

"You're the son? Cain? Abel? Uranus? Just one fuck's opinion but
how do you know I wish to remember his life with you?
His life with you? Those sorryass details? His petty days.
Maybe I don't want to justify input terminals drilled into my
skull? Do you know what it's like to have parasites and
bacteria injected into your brain—while you're still whistling
reveille like the Right Reverend?"

"Sorry.
No, I don't know
    that pain."

"Gorillas spend their days eating, consuming a diet of green
    leaves, stems, pork rinds, shoots, and red Slurpees. They
    travel to detox, between feedings, covering distances of
    several hundred yards to miles, miles a year. In lowland
    forests of east L.A. and Vegas gorillas drink substantial
    amounts of fruit daiquiris and so-so Beaujolais. The slow
    passage of pot seeds through their digestive tracts serves
    a hep-cat ecological process: the widespread dispersal and
    propagation of bullshit."

(Dad!)—
    was I allowed
        to laugh? Just one pink giggle?

"I've never been to the jungle, except through your father's head.
    He went to West Africa with your mother, on a photo safari.
    Honeymoon. We sexed two, three times a day. Once, in a
    stolen balloon. Below a half-dozen giraffe and gazelles,
    a rhino with a brass Ornette, toy villages, and a dog herding
    a cache of cattle, rogue elephants and a leopard, yes, yes,
    dangerous—so we sexed."

What's worse? Hearing
    your father brag about fucking
        your mother, or hearing

a gorilla wax
    about fucking your mother?
        He kicks the water.

"From that high loving, is you—you were made in the air. Isaac?"

"Yeah, the son," I say.
    I try not to stare.
        I've watched enough nature TV to know better.

"Crouch next to me, to our water. One schmuck's opinion but
    why did I name you Isaac?" I shrug. "Over there! I smell
    you! I smell you!" Another patient stands in the entranceway
    from the shower room, a towel wrapped around his head
    like a turban. He shifts his weight from leg to leg. "Stinky,
    stinky pink-skin come swim. The water's warm as hippo
    shit! I no eat you like croc-croc, I promise. Ha! I'll just
    chomp off your useless dick. You'll like that. That's more
    action than you've seen in ten years. Chomp-chomp,
    Farinelli! Come to my watering hole. My piss is peachy-
    keen! It's pumpkin-humpin'! It's lemony-anemone!"

The other patient backs away,
      back into the reptile steam.
         My gorilla fists his chest.

"You are named after Isaac Newton. When I was a kid I threw
      shit at people. You know? I had a favorite walnut tree. Sat
      up there for hours, cracking jokes, nuts and throwing shit at
      people. They'd look up like God it-self had shat on their day.
      Sad frown faces. That's power. Reminded me of when I
      reading a big book about discoverers, originals, like Isaac
      and Archimedes and Euclid and Marie. I loved that book.
      And another book about a jungle where I learned what I
      was—an ape—a tailless primate—a mimic—an idiot. I
      wanted to be like *them*. To invent! To create. I sent away
      for one of those rip-off kits sold on insomnia TV that
      teaches you how to patent your great ideas. Trouble was,
      I never had any great ideas. Not of my own. Never my own.
      I wrote trash. I helped make you: You: great. So I named you
      Isaac. Our life in you."

"Tell me about Mom.
      How did she die?
         What was she really like?

How come you never
      sent for me?"
         The gorilla stands,

situates
      and spreads his arms
         like Baron Scarpia, ready to deliver a sloppy one.

"Meanwhile, here in the Hotel Pedro, the reggae streams the
      velour-lit lobby as I lobby the manager for a bit of leeway in
      the ixnay. I'm weeks away from wrapping my new teleplay, an

adaptation of *Gravity's Rainbow*—with Terry Malick directing. Then the gravitas gravy train will toot-toot. The home range in which gorillas move, sleep and eat varies from 5 to 30 square kilometers. Whatever sinks your boat, as my sponsor used to say. However, research and tourist programs in the wild indicate that gorillas demonstrate extreme tolerance of *people* as long as *people* approach them respectfully. Sons are people, son. Are you poaching me, son, with all due respect? With *nous responsum*? The past isn't what it used to be.

"I recall riots, mudslides, earthquakes, mid-season cancellations, Manson and bi-lingual inquisitions, Fonda on Fonda, camouflage dildos, El Niño, freeway tag between sedans soused with cock rock shocks, Joe Friday, Sandy Koufax, locusts, fire, a white Bronto rising from the tar-pits and stampeding Wilshire, Bacchae-a-go-go, and a dozen wannabe Hockneys dosing in breeding pools reflecting platinum stars. Son, I wrote tragedies that no man will ever read!

"In some regions leopards have been known to attack gorillas. If you see spots before your eyes—it's too late.

"We stuffed our Speedos with pages of Didion! Your mother was born in an idiom too small for a drugstore. How to be, discovered? I was born in Ohiowa and came west to write the great American play. Remember that chapter of *Bewitched* where Darren dons Bjork's swan-dress and beak to defile a girl who believes she's Leda? That was my work! I was nominated for a late night Emmy. Years played out. My wife died. I may have sold policy? Dick Yorick told me, 'Heaven is where they screen the made-for-TV version of your life. In Hell they lock you in the cutting room, with

a candle and they make you watch the rest, the other 99%,
cell by cell.' The Hotelier and me worked a deal—my signed
Sonny Chiba glossy for 30 more days.

"The revolution isolates me. I'd give the world from narcolepsy
to narcotic for one more season. The Chinese can't tell me
from you. I've tasted. I've asked:

"Isaac—

"I was in Mexico with another woman when your mother died.
I don't know what happened to her. It's a tragedy. Who
was she with? Who was I with? Why jump? Over me? Over
my infidelity? I'm sorry, son. I failed. I failed our tribe.
When The People's Army descends from the Alps with their
attack pandas I'll be sunning, by this pool, my laptop
humming, browsing the sky for crop dusters and rain.

"Son, do you smell our love?"

"Yes, Dad. I do."
I put my hand on his shoulder.
He makes a sound

between smithereens and merciless goddamned beauty.
He takes my hand
and puts the whole unit,

all five digits, into his mouth.
When he lets my hand
out

it's purple
like a mountain,
like Niobe's heart.

"Oedipus is already eye-balled. Remember I am gigantic—
Leviathan—twisted, coiled. I'm a knuckle-walker. I'm a
tribe of hairy women. If threatened—I defend my band
by roaring, screaming obscenities, beating my chest with
cupped hands. I am against the designated driver. I like
Harold Lloyd. At dusk a family should settle where it has
finished feeding. We will build our yurts on the ground or in
a tree, by bending nearby vegetation to form a flexible
platforms and monograms.

"I will charge, if the threat is serious.

"A father protects his children—Antigonê, Ismenê, Eteoclês, and
Polyneicês—history is hence. I will plunge toward my
enemy, with impudicity, with brass balls flying—

"love is a hazardous art."

10

At the train station, I lean
        against a billboard
                advertising truth serum.

I think of my gorilla's face
        as they led him
                into the lab. I gulp

from a paper sack. I smell feral.
        I think local.
                I let another engine

run my brain from my heart.
        I hear music.
                Then I hear music.

I follow the sound
    to find a blind man
        dressed in turtle-shell Ray-Bans
and a crimson jalabiyya.
    It's the king!—
        playing a natural-blonde
Model 325 Rickenbacker
    with a Kauffman vibrato.
    His feet
are set in cement blocks. He sings
    with a voice stained
        with dead roses:

      You can't sing like a God
        'til you've been kicked
          like a dog.
      You can't soar with the Roc
        'til you've been trussed
          like a sold hog.
    It's more the way it's now
        than it will ever be before.
        Oh, General Ike!
    It's more the way it's now
        than it will ever be before.
        Oh, Mr. Yessir!

    You can't rest down cloud nine
        'til you've been burned
          like a hewn vine.
    You can't learn to divine
        'til you've been blinded
          by moonshine.

It's more the way it's now
than it will ever be before.
Oh, General Ike!
It's more the way it's now
than it will ever be before.
Oh, Mr. Yessir!

He bows and I empty my pocket
into his hat. My train arrives
and back home

taped to the fire escape I find
an eviction notice.
What with the new political realities, Pok

can't afford to have a tenant like me.
I'm not surprised.
My chest is too sore to pound

and my voice is too sore to foreswear.
She stuffed all my clothes
into a black plastic garbage bag.

One bag.
I can live light. I'm not anxious. No,
I'm ready for my cue.

Tomorrow I'll have to begin saving
my father.
Isn't that what a son does

when his old man has been transformed into a mountain gorilla?
I climb
to the roof. It's a warm night.

I look down through the hole
        into my old room. Yaz stands
            on my bed, my pillow

is in her mouth. She's sovereign, now.
        The mask over my face melts.
            Halloween

                    lights reflect and puddle
clogging the storm drains.
        In the distance I see the palmful of water
            inside the sea:

                the syntax.

I hear voices—a muffled chorus.
        Mr. Pok's Christmas cards are playing
            for the moles:

Hark how the bells, sweet silver bells,
        all seem to say throw cares away....
            on on they send, on without end,

                    their joyful tone to every home—

I lay back on my back to watch
        the twisted stars
            tremble as I absent

                without leave.

A Note About the Type

This book is set in a digital version of Rudolph Ruzicka's Fairfield. Ruzicka, a Czech-born American, designed Fairfield in 1940 for the Mergenthaler Linotype Company, then under the guidance of Chauncey H. Griffith. Fairfield was originally designed in only two weights with italics: Light, released in 1940, and Medium, released in 1947. In 1991, type designer Alex Kaczun added bold, heavy, small caps, old-style figures, swash caps and caption typefaces to the digital Fairfield family.

Fairfield was designed very simply with the reader in mind; a reader who, in Ruzicka's own words, "expects nothing but to be left in optical ease while he pursues his reading—he wants no interruptions of the process of following the printed thought." While maintaining old-style characteristics, Fairfield's decorative flourishes can be attributed to its long ascenders, modestly contrasting thick to thin strokes and unbracketed serifs.